CATHOLICS
AND
FUNDAMENTALISTS
WHAT'S THE DIFFERENCE?

By Father Martin Pable, OFM Cap.

HI-TIME Publishing Corp.
Box 13337
Milwaukee, WI 53213-0337

Nihil Obstat: Reverend Monsignor John F. Murphy,
Censor Librorum
January 30, 1991
Imprimatur: Most Reverend Rembert G. Weakland, O.S.B.,
Archbishop of Milwaukee
February 1, 1991

PHOTO CREDITS

The Crosiers/Gene Plaisted — pages 14, 19, 21, 26, 37, 42, 57
Jack Hamilton — pages 9, 24, 44, 51, 61
Skjold Photographs — page 32

HI-TIME Publishing Corp.
P.O. Box 13337
Milwaukee, WI 53213-0337

Library of Congress Catalog Card Number 91-70460
ISBN 0-937997-18-8

Contents

Preface

For the past twenty-five years Catholics have been working hard to further the process of Church renewal inaugurated by the Second Vatican Council. Dramatic changes in the Liturgy, a new approach to religious education, greater participation of the laity in parish administration — all have moved forward despite fears, mistakes, and uncertainties.

But just when these efforts to bring Church teachings and structures into line with modern times seem to be taken for granted, a new phenomenon has burst upon Catholics: the challenge of the Fundamentalist churches. For a number of years I watched while large numbers of Catholics, especially younger ones, left their Church for one of the Fundamentalist churches, creating hurt, anger, and confusion among their families and friends.

Sometime ago I decided to do something besides watch. I began to do a great deal of reading and listening to people who have studied or experienced membership in Fundamentalist churches, including some Catholics who joined and later left. Then, four years ago, I began offering seminars on "A Catholic Response to Fundamentalism" at Sacred Heart School of Theology in Hales Corners, Wisconsin. These seminars were well received, and later I was encouraged to put the material into book form.

I wanted to write something fairly brief and easy to comprehend, something that could be read and understood by those who are puzzled by Fundamentalist arguments and attacks on Catholic beliefs. I have tried to be fair to the Fundamentalist positions in the hope that some Fundamentalists may be disposed to hear both sides of a question.

It is my hope that all Christians will continue to seek the person of Jesus Christ and His message in all aspects of their lives. I am especially grateful to the students in my classes, whose insights and questions were so helpful in the writing of this book.

Father Martin Pable, OFM Cap.
October 4, 1990
Feast of St. Francis of Assisi

CHAPTER ONE

What Is Fundamentalism?

A few years ago in *New Catholic World,* Father Thomas Stransky related the following story. Two Catholic parents, active participants in the area's adult religious education program, sought his advice in their bewilderment. "Ten years ago," they said, "one of our children returned from the state university, proclaimed that God was dead and so was all our 'church stuff.' He remains an agnostic. Now our youngest has come back for the summer break and is preaching that we parents are damned because we are not truly committed to Jesus and are not Bible-believing Christians. She calls herself a Fundamentalist." They concluded: "Agnostics we understand. Some of those Eastern cults we have studied. But Fundamentalists — what are they about?"

This kind of scene is being enacted in thousands of Catholic homes across America today. It is a heartbreaking experience for sincere parents who have tried to give their children a good Catholic upbringing. While adolescents and young adults are particularly susceptible to the influence of Fundamentalist churches, a number of older Catholics are also joining the ranks. And among traditionally Catholic Hispanics, the drift toward Fundamentalist churches is nothing short of alarming. Bishop Ricardo Ramirez of Las Cruces, New Mexico, has predicted that the Catholic Church could lose as many as twenty million members by the end of the century.

What are we to think of all this? It would be easy to react with blame, anger, or guilt. Catholic parents tend to blame themselves when their sons or daughters go over to a Fundamentalist church. Other Catholics are angry at these churches for their "sheep-stealing" tactics. Particularly on secular college campuses, Fundamentalist groups like Inter-Varsity and Navigators are trained to spot lonely or insecure young Catholics, befriend them, and invite them to their socials and Bible study sessions. Soon they begin to challenge the Catholic's beliefs until he or she repudiates them in favor of the simple slogans of the Fundamentalists.

Still other Catholics blame the Church for failing to equip our people with an adequate knowledge of the Faith and of the Bible. And those who are more theologically sophisticated find it easy to poke holes in the Fundamentalist positions.

But I don't find any of these reactions to be particularly helpful. Guilt and blame only tend to paralyze constructive analysis and action. Anger is not useful unless it can create positive energy. Attacking the Fundamentalists' weak intellectual foundations may bring us some satisfaction, but it will not lessen their emotional appeal to dissatisfied Catholics.

I believe we need to take the Fundamentalist challenge seriously. This does not mean adopting a defensive or negative

Particularly on college campuses, Fundamentalists are active.

posture. Rather, the situation calls for understanding, for careful analysis, for critical reflection and positive response. This is what I hope to offer in this book.

Origins of Fundamentalism

Fundamentalism is not the same as traditionalism or conservatism. Traditionalist tendencies are present in every major religion. Present-day Fundamentalism began as a reaction to major intellectual upheavals in the late nineteenth century. In biology, the evolutionary theory of Charles Darwin seemed to contradict the biblical accounts of creation by postulating that the earth gradually evolved over a period of millions of years, and that humans themselves had evolved from lower forms of life. In psychology, Sigmund Freud claimed that human freedom of will is an illusion, that our choices are really determined by unconscious motives and dynamisms buried deep in our psyche. Karl Marx was claiming that religion is a creation of the ruling classes to maintain control over the working classes and the poor: "Don't worry if you have to suffer in this life; you will be rewarded in the life to come."

In response to these attacks on traditional religion, some liberal Protestant scholars tried to make some accommodation to the new scientific thinking. They began to study the Bible more critically, taking into account the various literary forms in which the Bible was written, as well as the findings of archaeology and cultural anthropology. They concluded that not all the biblical accounts had to be understood literally, that evolution did not necessarily contradict the Scriptures, and that some of the biblical truths were open to various interpretations.

In reaction to these ideas, some conservative Protestant scholars wrote a series of booklets, between 1910 and 1915, called *The Fundamentals*. In the series they rejected the "modernist" attempts to accommodate Christian teaching to the claims of science. They insisted on strict adherence to a number of doctrinal points, the main ones being:

1) the absolute inspiration and inerrancy of the words of the Bible;
2) the virginal birth and divinity of Jesus Christ;
3) the substitutionary atonement for our sins through Christ's death on the cross;
4) the bodily resurrection of Christ;
5) the literal Second Coming of Christ at the end of time.

At first glance, most Catholics would feel "at home" with these points, especially numbers two, four and five. We, too, believe that Jesus Christ is truly divine as well as human, that He physically rose from the dead, and that He will return in glory at the end of time. It is points one and three that create the most tension between Catholics and Fundamentalists. While Fundamentalists insist that the very words of the Bible must be taken literally, most Catholics allow for some interpretation of the biblical texts. Regarding the substitutionary atonement, Fundamentalists claim that Catholics deny the sufficiency of Christ's death for our salvation because we believe in the efficacy of "good works" such as the Mass and the sacraments. We shall also examine point number five, since the Fundamentalist interpretation of the Second Coming of Christ involves notions of "the millennium" and "the rapture," ideas which are not familiar to most Catholics.

Of course, there are a variety of Fundamentalist churches. There are the "Assemblies of God," the "Church of Christ" of Boston, Milwaukee, and so on, "Full Gospel" churches, and many others with names such as "Church of the Good Shepherd" or "Calvary Temple." They may differ among themselves in some respects, but all will hold to the five "Fundamentals" described above.

The Appeal of Fundamentalism

While overall membership in Fundamentalist churches is not large, they are the fastest-growing churches in America today. The question naturally comes to mind: What is their appeal? And why are so many Catholics seemingly attracted to them? A good understanding of this question will enable us to formulate some helpful pastoral responses to the Fundamentalist challenge.

In general, the appeal of Fundamentalism lies in its simplicity. Many Catholics today are confused by the differences of opinion and practice among theologians, pastors, and ordinary members of the Church. It is difficult at times to know who or what to believe. In place of all this, Fundamentalist preachers and believers present a simple message that promises certainty of salvation. The basic outlines are as follows.

In the first place, Fundamentalists put their confidence not in any human person or organization, but in the authority of the Bible. The word of God is their sole rule of faith, and it is to be taken literally. The Bible teaches clearly that human beings are sinners, utterly incapable of saving themselves or gaining eternal life by their own efforts. Our situation would be hopeless unless God intervened. But the good news is: God in His mercy sent His son Jesus into the world to die for our sins. Because Jesus was both divine and human, His death had infinite value and power to wash away all our sins once and for all.

But in order for this salvation to touch us personally, there is one (and only one) thing we have to do: Confess our sinfulness and helplessness and invite Jesus Christ into our hearts as our personal Savior. This is what it means to be "born again." It is not accomplished through some external ritual such as Baptism (and certainly not infant Baptism). Rather, it must be a personal decision arising out of a conviction of one's utter need for a Savior. And once I have made that act of surrender, I am absolutely certain of my salvation. Even my subsequent sins cannot invalidate that basic decision, so long as I continue to believe in the power of Christ to save me.

As we can well imagine, Fundamentalists find profound peace and liberation in this belief system. Whatever doubts they may have — about the future of the economy, or their health, or the condition of the world — they have absolute certainty about the one thing that matters: their eternal salva-

tion. They know they are going to heaven. This is why Fundamentalists are genuinely puzzled when they ask a Catholic,
"Are you saved?" — and the Catholic answers, "Well, I think
so. I hope so." To the Fundamentalist, that sounds like doubt
about the saving action of Jesus Christ. More about this later.

Another appealing aspect of Fundamentalism is that its
members generally appear to embody traditional and family-
oriented values. Many Fundamentalists attend church services
at least twice a week. They are devoted to Bible study. Their
children attend classes on the Bible and are instructed on how
to witness for Christ. Fundamentalist believers project a positive, cheerful attitude toward life. They are warm and friendly,
often the first ones to offer help in time of need. On college
campuses, Fundamentalist students are clean-cut and out-
going, have high moral standards, and still know how to have a
good time. If you are a stranger at their church services or
social gatherings, you will be warmly welcomed, introduced to
everyone, and made to feel at home. For many Catholics, this
is in sharp contrast to what they have experienced in the large,
impersonal settings of their own parish churches.

Finally, Fundamentalists are encouraged and trained to
be evangelizers. They consider it their mission to go out and
save others for Christ. Many Catholics, of course, resent it
when Fundamentalists badger them with questions like "Do
you know the Lord?" or "Are you a born-again Christian?"
Still, it is hard not to admire that kind of zeal and courage, or
to wonder why it is not more common in the Catholic Church.

The Darker Side

However, along with the appeal of Fundamentalism is a
darker side that many Catholics perceive only later. One form
it takes is a certain arrogance or smugness. Fundamentalists
are not only certain of their own salvation; they have little
hope for anyone else's. If you do not believe as they do, you
cannot be saved.

For some curious reasons I do not understand, Fundamentalists seem especially anxious to convert Catholics. Perhaps they perceive us as the most deceived and blinded of all Christians, in critical danger of losing our souls. At any rate, Fundamentalist criticisms of Catholic beliefs follow a standard pattern: We do not know the Bible or use it as our norm of faith; we do not accept Jesus Christ as our only Savior; we put our faith in human sources such as Mary and the saints, sacraments, rituals, prayers, and the pope; we trust more in our own works than in the cross of Christ to save us.

Sometimes, though, the criticisms take a harsh and vicious form. I have found Fundamentalist pamphlets on my car window calling upon Catholics to renounce their "damnable" beliefs and practices and their "devilish" rituals, so that they can be saved from the fires of hell. Sister Mary Frances Reis, in her article, "Fundamentalism on the College Campus," quotes a Catholic student as saying, "I came to Mass today (November 1), though it was the hardest thing I ever did. My roommates kept yelling at me and saying I was going to hell because I came to worship the saints." Another student, a former Catholic, tells her friends, "My mom and dad are going to hell. I tried to save them, but they wouldn't join my church."

I have spoken with families who have had to listen to bitter and hateful accusations like this from their own members. It is impossible for me to see how this can be the fruit of grace or the Holy Spirit. At the very least it contradicts the

Fundamentalists seem especially anxious to convert Catholics.

Bible's teaching on the mercy of God, who wants all to be saved (1 Timothy 2:4).

Another dark side of Fundamentalism is its separatism and elitism. Their literature often proclaims that "we do not have fellowship with unbelievers." "Unbelievers" apparently means anyone who does not believe in their brand of Christianity. That is why most Fundamentalist churches will not work ecumenically with "mainline" Protestant and Catholic churches. To do so, presumably, would be to risk cooperating in the works of Satan. It is this kind of black-and-white thinking that often turns away Catholics who have felt some initial attraction to a Fundamentalist church.

Finally, there is a strange irony in the Fundamentalist belief system. On the one hand, they claim that God's word in the Bible is their sole authority; any kind of human authority or hierarchy is contrary to the mind of Christ. However, when someone begins to question one of the Fundamentalist teachings or interpretations of Scripture, he or she is promptly warned about the danger of wandering into the camp of Satan. And if the member dares to leave the church, the member is made to feel that he or she has chosen the path to hell. There are numerous stories about people who have experienced severe guilt feelings after leaving a Fundamentalist church. There is even a support group called "Fundamentalists Anonymous" to help people deal with the internal stress and external harassment they encounter in leaving the church. This kind of heavy-handed authoritarianism is another dark side of Fundamentalism.

CHAPTER TWO

Fundamentalism and the Bible

There is no doubt that the cornerstone of Fundamentalist teaching and preaching is the Bible. Indeed, Fundamentalists pride themselves on being "Bible-believing" Christians. But since all Christians (as well as Jews) accept the authority of the Scriptures, Fundamentalists obviously have something special in mind when they say "Bible-believing": They mean understanding the Bible literally. In his book *Evangelicalism: The Coming Generation,* James Hunter quotes a college student as saying, "If the Bible isn't true, everything in my life would be so tentative. I think there would be no rock to go back to. Why hold so tightly to my faith if it is not even stable?"

Not only is the Bible a true and stable source of truth, it is also easy to understand, according to Fundamentalists. They are fond of quoting one of their own scholars, Charles Hodge: "The Bible is a plain book. It is intelligible by the people. And they have the right and are bound to read and interpret it for themselves; so that their faith may rest on the testimony of the Scriptures, and not that of the Church."

Because the Bible is the word of God, it must be believed. And because it is a "plain" book, it does not have to be interpreted by experts or authorities; it can be understood by "plain" people if they read it plainly — that is, literally. All that is required is that it be read with faith and with prayer for the guidance of the Holy Spirit.

However, it soon becomes obvious that one runs into all sorts of problems when one begins to read the Bible literally — that is, without trying to interpret its meaning. For example, what does the Book of Genesis mean when it says that God created the heavens and the earth in six days? Or what does Jesus mean when He says, "From the days of John the Baptist until now, the kingdom of heaven suffers violence, and the violent are taking it by force" (Matthew 11:12)?

Not only are some passages in the Bible very obscure; there are also outright contradictions in some of the texts. Matthew's account of the Beatitudes says that Jesus "went up the mountain," His disciples gathered around Him, and He taught them at length, beginning with eight Beatitudes (Matthew 5:1). In Luke's account, Jesus "came down with them and stood on a stretch of level ground" (Luke 6:17) and taught the crowd, beginning with four Beatitudes. Which account is true? Was it a "Sermon on the Mount" or a "Sermon on the Plain"? Were there eight Beatitudes or four? And what about the famous passage in which Jesus tells the disciples, "Call no one on earth your father; you have but one Father in heaven" (Matthew 23:9)? Fundamentalists like to quote these words against Catholics who call their priest "Father." Yet it is clear from later New Testament writings that Christians continued to call their parents "father" and "mother." The First Letter of John says, "I am writing to you, fathers, because you know

---

What does the Bible mean when it says that God created the heavens and the earth in six days?

him who is from the beginning" (1 John 2:13). And Paul writes, "Even if you should have countless guides to Christ, yet you do not have many fathers, for I became your father in Christ Jesus through the gospel" (1 Corinthians 4:15). So even Paul calls himself "father." Either the inspired writers were being disobedient to Christ — which is unthinkable — or Christ's words have to be understood other than literally.

Moreover, if the words of the Bible are to be taken plainly and literally, why don't Fundamentalists wash each other's feet or invite the poor, the lame and the blind to their lunches and dinners — since this is plainly what Jesus asks of His disciples (John 13:14; Luke 14:12-13)?

The point is, the Bible is not as plain and simple as the Fundamentalists would like to believe. As a matter of fact, when they are pressed, they will admit that the Bible needs to be interpreted. Accordingly, their scholars have worked to produce lengthy "commentaries" on the biblical books. One of the most popular today is the *Liberty Commentary on the New Testament,* edited by Jerry Falwell. Even more influential is the famous *Scofield Reference Bible,* written by C.I. Scofield, and its updated version, *The New Scofield Reference Bible.*

The purpose of the commentaries is to help the Christian understand the true meaning of the Bible. Fundamentalists claim that the devout reader can understand the text with the help of the Holy Spirit; still, they recognize the danger of every reader's interpreting the text in his or her own way, which would result in biblical anarchy.

The problem is, the commentaries are not widely circulated among ordinary Fundamentalist Christians. They are used mainly by the pastors and preachers. Moreover, there is often disagreement among the commentators themselves. For

What did Jesus mean when He said, "Call no one on earth your father . . ."?

example, the Book of Revelation describes a version of 200 million horses and riders bringing plagues to the earth (Revelation 9:13-19). The horses have a fantastic appearance: tails like snakes and heads like those of lions breathing out fire, smoke, and sulphur. They are sent to destroy one-third of the human race. Now, how is this vision to be interpreted? One Fundamentalist commentator, Oliver Greene, says that the horses must be understood as some kind of supernatural beings. On the other hand, Leon Bates calls them "vehicles" that kill by fire, smoke, and "projectiles"; hence, they may be the equivalent of modern missile-launching tanks. And finally, Hal Lindsey claims the passage is a prophecy of modern nuclear war!

What is the Christian Bible reader to think? Where can he or she turn for an authoritative interpretation of a puzzling passage? Fundamentalists answer, "To the pastor." Richard De Haan, of the Radio Bible Class, explains the close connection between the pastor and the biblical text: "Yes, he is a fallible human being, but God has entrusted His infallible word to that man. He therefore has a great message to proclaim, and you are under obligation to heed the exhortations and obey the directives which come from the Scriptures through the pastor to you" (*Your Pastor and You,* p. 18; quoted in Kathleen Boone, *The Bible Tells Them So: The Discourse of Protestant Fundamentalism.* (See **Bibliography**.) Or, as Jerry Falwell likes to put it, the pastor is "God's man," and, therefore, his directives are to be obeyed by the Christian disciple.

So now we have come full circle. The Fundamentalists begin with the claim that the Bible is inspired by God and cannot contain error. It is a plain book that can be understood by plain people who read it with faith; the believer is guided by the Holy Spirit, so there is no need for church authority. Yet the believers are not allowed to interpret the text any way they choose. If they do not have access to the approved commentaries, they are to submit their questions and even their views to the authority of the pastor. In his study of a Fundamentalist Christian school, Alan Peshkin quotes a student disgruntled with the quality of church music: "The Bible distinctly says, you know, take trumpets and cymbals and stuff and praise the Lord with that. Over here in _____ , if you don't have just a piano or organ, it's wrong, it's a sin. . . ." It is ironic that some Catholics who left the Church because they found it too authoritarian are willing to accept an even more rigid authority structure in a Fundamentalist church.

Place of the Bible in the Catholic Church

By this time the reader might be thinking, "Well, if the Fundamentalist view of the Bible is flawed, what is the Catholic view? And how is it different?"

In the first place, Catholics agree that the Bible is the inspired word of God. The Second Vatican Council states that all the books of the Old and New Testaments are sacred because they "have been written down under the inspiration of the Holy Spirit. . . . they have God as their author" (*Dogmatic Constitution on Divine Revelation,* article 11).

However, we must not think of God as "author" in the sense that He "dictated" the whole Bible word for word. Rather, as the council says, God chose human writers and "made full use of their powers and faculties so that, though he acted in them and by them, it was as true authors that they consigned to writing whatever he wanted written, and no more" *(Ibid.).* The Church takes this notion of human authorship very seriously. The council goes on to encourage biblical scholars to study the historical and cultural circumstances in which the various books were composed — as well as their literary form — in order to understand them better. It also states that any biblical passage must not be taken in isolation or out of context, but must be read and interpreted in light of the Bible as a whole.

As long ago as 1943, Pope Pius XII encouraged Catholic biblical scholars to study the sacred texts in their original languages and within the context of their cultural and literary expressions. The Church, he said, has nothing to fear from this kind of scientific study of the Bible; on the contrary, it can vastly enrich our understanding of God's word. Fundamentalists, on the other hand, reject this approach to the Bible as a

dangerous kind of "modernism" that will undermine the faith of Christians.

This leads us to the question of biblical "inerrancy," a point on which Fundamentalists and Catholics also differ. Fundamentalists insist that the Bible is absolutely free of error. If it states that God made Adam out of the clay of the earth and Eve out of Adam's rib, it must be so; if it says that the sun stood still in the sky for a whole day, or that Jonah was in the fish's belly for three days, it must be so. For if the Bible is "wrong" on **any** matter, how can we be sure it is true about anything, including the death or resurrection of Christ?

The Catholic Church also teaches that the Bible is without error, but with this important difference: "Inerrancy" extends only to the **religious** truths of the Bible, those which are necessary or important for our spiritual life and eternal salvation. There may well be scientific or historical errors in the Bible, as well as literary exaggerations; but these in no way diminish our faith in the Bible as the source of religious truth. The sacred writers were simply not interested in teaching science, history or psychology. They accepted the common views of their time and culture, and God guided them in their task of recording His wonderful deeds and teaching His wise ways for the spiritual good of the human race.

So, for example, Catholics would find no contradiction between the creation accounts in Genesis and the gradual formation of the universe over millions of years — or even the evolution of the human species. Genesis is simply teaching the profound religious truth that God is the ultimate Source and Creator of all that exists, that He guided in a wondrous manner the forces that shaped our universe and allowed for the evolution of the species. Likewise, it is no threat to our faith when contemporary Scripture scholars say that the Book of

---

Fundamentalists claim that individual readers can understand the Bible with the help of the Holy Spirit.

Jonah is most likely not a "true" historical account; rather, it is a parable (much like the Good Samaritan story in the Gospel) that teaches a beautiful religious truth: God's willingness to forgive even pagan peoples who turn to Him in repentance.

The major point we are making is this: The Bible is not always a "plain" book, any more than Shakespeare's plays are "plain." The ordinary reader can always find inspiration and guidance from reading it prayerfully, just as he or she can gain insight into human nature by reading Shakespeare. But because the Bible can too easily be misunderstood, it needs (at least sometimes) to be clarified and interpreted. It is interesting that this need for help in interpretation is expressed in the Bible itself. When the Ethiopian official was reading the prophet Isaiah, Philip the deacon asked him, "Do you understand what you are reading?" And the man replied, "How can I, unless someone instructs me?" (Acts 8:30-31). Similarly, Catholics have always felt the need for some guidance in reading the Scriptures, because of the all-too-human tendency to misinterpret and misunderstand. One of the letters of Peter also warns about this tendency. Speaking of Paul's letters he says, "In them there are some things hard to understand that the ignorant and unstable distort to their own destruction, just as they do the other scriptures" (2 Peter 3:16).

How, then, do Catholics hope to avoid the pitfalls of misunderstanding or distorting the meaning of the Bible? For one thing, like the Fundamentalists, we depend on the Holy Spirit's guidance, which we seek in prayer. We believe that God truly does speak to us, enlighten us, comfort us and challenge us when we read His word prayerfully. At the same time, we take care not to isolate the Bible from the ongoing life of the Church or from our spiritual life as a whole. Our reading of the Bible is not a strictly private matter; we want to do it

---

Every time Catholics gather for worship, the Church gives a prominent place to the reading of God's word.

within the context of the Christian community. That is what we Catholics mean by "tradition."

"Tradition" is simply the set of beliefs held by the Christian community and handed down by word of mouth from one generation to the next. An important truth often forgotten by both Catholics and Fundamentalists is that the community we call "the Church" was in existence long before the book we know as "the Bible" came to be. As someone once put it, "It was the Church that gave us the Bible, not the other way around."

Which leads to an interesting question: How, then, was the Bible formed? First, it is crucial to remember that God has revealed Himself to us primarily through His **actions** in history: creation, the call of Abraham, the exodus of the Jewish people from slavery, the covenant between them and God on Mount Sinai, the exile and homecoming of the people, and, finally, the life, death and resurrection of Jesus and the outpouring of the Holy Spirit upon the new people of God, the Christian community. Long before these events were written down, the people remembered these wonderful deeds of God and recounted them for their children. Eventually, various authors wrote them down, under divine inspiration, so that there would be no substantial errors.

The same basic pattern was followed for the New Testament. The stories about the life and teachings of Jesus were handed on by word of mouth. People in those days were used to remembering and recounting stories accurately. In fact, there was no written "Gospel" until about three decades after the resurrection. Luke, who wrote his Gospel around 80-85 A.D., clearly says in his prologue that his material was "handed down" to him by "eyewitnesses . . . and ministers of the word" (Luke 1:2). By this time, the letters of Paul, John, and Peter were also being circulated among the Christians.

The problem was that many other writings — some of them quite popular and inspirational — were also making their way around. So eventually the question had to be addressed: Which of these are "inspired" (and therefore "Scripture") and which are not? Remember, there was no "Bible" as yet. It had not even been decided which of the Old Testament writings were to be regarded as inspired. And who had the authority to decide such important questions? History gives us the answer: It was **the community** — especially "the elders" (presbyters and bishops) — who would gather in councils to prayerfully discern which of these writings were in harmony with the oral tradition that had been handed on through previous generations. And our belief (Protestants as well as Catholics) is that the Church community was guided by the Holy Spirit in these decisions. So it was not until near the end of the fourth century that Church councils gave final approval to the present books of the Bible.

This, I think, would raise a troubling question for Fundamentalists: If the Bible is the sole guide for faith and salvation, how could people believe and be saved before there was a Bible?

At any rate, Catholics believe that since the Bible grew out of the believing community, under the inspiration of the Holy Spirit, it must be read and interpreted with the help of the community. We have already seen that Fundamentalists also rely on the community to help them understand the Bible; they make use of commentaries or consult their pastors. Catholics do the same, the difference being that they have the benefit of two thousand years of the Church community's study, reflection and scholarship, as well the authoritative teaching of popes and councils. The Bible cannot be separated from tradition or from the teaching authority of the pope and bishops. In the early Church, as we have seen, all three "grew up" together.

Fundamentalists often accuse Catholics of ignoring the Bible. There may have been some truth to this charge in the past; certainly, Catholics were not given much encouragement to read the Bible. But today this is no longer valid. The Second Vatican Council insisted that "all the preaching of the Church, as indeed the entire Christian religion, should be nourished and ruled by Sacred Scripture" (*Dogmatic Constitution on Divine Revelation,* article 21). This is why, every time we gather for worship — whether for Mass, the sacraments, or public devotions — the Church gives a prominent place to the reading of God's word.

Moreover, the Second Vatican Council went on to encourage individual Catholics to read the Scriptures: "Likewise, the sacred Synod forcefully and specifically exhorts all the Christian faithful . . . to learn 'the surpassing knowledge of Jesus Christ' (Phil. 3:8) by frequent reading of the divine Scriptures." For, as Saint Jerome says, "Ignorance of the Scriptures is ignorance of Christ." Then the Council reminds us that our reading should always be accompanied by prayer. And it quotes the beautiful saying of Saint Ambrose: "we speak to him [God] when we pray; we listen to him [God] when we read the divine oracles" (*Dogmatic Constitution on Divine Revelation,* article 25).

Perhaps the Catholic attitude toward the Bible can be summed up in three simple sentences:

"When I read the Scriptures, I believe I am reading the word of God — I will find spiritual nourishment and guidance for my life."
"But I will always try to understand the Bible in light of its **whole** message, and be careful not to take the words out of their context."
"And when something in the Bible seems puzzling, or I don't understand it, I believe I can be helped by the insights of Church authorities and scholars who have made a special study of the Bible."

Catholics and Fundamentalists share a common love for the Bible, although they differ on how it should be used. We turn now to another important issue: the meaning of *salvation.*

CHAPTER THREE

"Are You Saved?"

If you have ever had the experience of talking to a Fundamentalist, he or she will eventually pop the question, "Are you saved?" Anthony Gilles, in his book *Fundamentalism: What Every Catholic Needs To Know,* calls this "the jackpot question." It has a great deal of meaning to Fundamentalists, but Catholics usually find it puzzling. They don't know what to say.

Catholics and Fundamentalists share a fairly common understanding of the word *salvation.* It means that in Jesus Christ, God has forgiven our sins, reconciled us to Himself in a bond of friendship and love, and given us a firm hope of eternal life in the world to come. This salvation is not our own achievement; it was won for us through the death and resurrection of Christ.

So far so good. The question remains, however: What is **our** part in salvation? The Bible is clear that God wants all people to be saved (1 Timothy 2:4). At the same time, God will not force salvation on us. God respects our free will, so we have the awesome capacity to either accept or reject salvation.

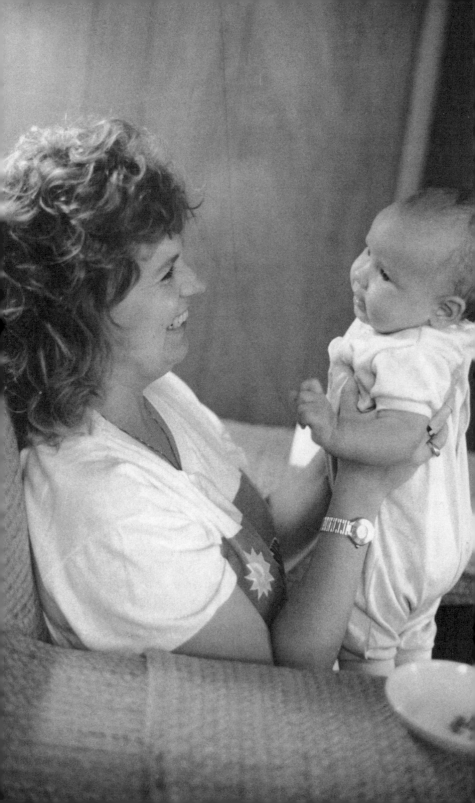

So the question becomes, How do we "take hold" of the salvation Christ has won for us? Fundamentalists answer, "When we make a personal decision to accept Jesus Christ as our Lord and Savior." The typical formula is, "Confess your sins and receive Him into your heart." In other words, in a moment of truth and grace, I come to the realization that I am on a downward path spiritually. Feeling the guilt and weight of my own sins (I can't keep blaming everyone else for my own failures), and feeling my utter powerlessness to turn my life around by my own efforts, I come to believe that Jesus Christ gave His life for me on the cross and thereby took away my sins once and for all. I don't have to keep trying so hard to be perfect; all I have to do is commit my life to Christ and let Him be my Savior. This is what it means to be "born again."

A number of consequences flow from this theology of salvation. Note, first of all, that the "saving act" is purely an internal one. There is no need for any external ritual or public ceremony. Some Fundamentalists do not even believe in the necessity of Baptism, except as an external sign of the great event that has taken place internally. And all Fundamentalists reject infant Baptism; they see it as a meaningless ritual, since the baby is incapable of making a conscious commitment to Christ.

Second, Fundamentalists believe that once they have made this decisive commitment, their salvation is absolutely assured. This is why they exude such spiritual self-confidence, and why they can't understand it when Catholics seem to "waffle" about their assurance of salvation: "Well, gee, I **hope** I'll be saved, but I suppose I can blow it if I'm not careful. . . ."

What do Fundamentalists mean when they talk about being "born again"?

Fundamentalists can't understand such talk. For them, once you accept Jesus Christ into your heart, He will never abandon you. Not even if you go back to a life of sin? No — your sins cannot invalidate your salvation. The only way you can be lost is to explicitly repudiate your act of commitment to Christ. The slogan is, "Once saved, always saved."

I once asked a Fundamentalist pastor about this: "Do you mean to say that if I give myself to Christ, but then live like a pagan, disregard the Commandments of God, and so on, I will still be saved in the end?" He answered by making a distinction between "salvation" and "retribution." Yes, salvation is once-for-all, because God is faithful to His promises. But I will certainly experience retribution: God will send me setbacks, failures, sickness, and so on, in an effort to bring me back to my senses. But no — I will not be lost unless I formally reject Jesus Christ.

This is certainly a comforting doctrine. But it strains credibility. Is suffering and sickness always a sign of divine retribution? The whole purpose of the Book of Job is to correct that wrong idea. And all of us know people who, like Job, are models of innocence and upright living — yet they suffer in innumerable ways. And on the other side, the world is full of drug dealers, con artists, Mafia-like gangsters, and so on, who are living like kings and queens with no evidence of divine retribution! And some of them claim to be "born-again Christians." One has to wonder if this kind of theology contributed to the downfall of some of the televangelists.

A third consequence of the Fundamentalist view of salvation is a narrow, exclusivist idea of who can or will be saved. For one thing, salvation is limited to those who accept Christ as their Savior — which excludes Jews, Moslems, and members of other non-Christian religions. Moreover, it is limited to Christians who have been "born again," who have surrendered their lives to Christ in the manner described above. Everyone else is literally on the road to hell. This is what accounts for the evangelistic fervor of Fundamentalists. They sincerely believe it is their mission to persuade as many people as possible to make a soul-saving decision for Christ. It also explains the darker side: their intolerance — sometimes bordering on fanaticism — of those who do not believe as they do.

Catholic View of Salvation

Well, how do Catholics view salvation? As we have seen, they agree with Fundamentalists that it is not a human achievement but God's work. But Catholics believe it is not a once-for-all event; rather, salvation is an ongoing process. In addition, it is not merely a private, interior experience of turning to the Lord; it includes the public, external rite of Baptism. Based on the Gospel of John, Catholics take Baptism very seriously. In chapter three, a Pharisee named Nicodemus comes to talk to Jesus, and Jesus tells him solemnly, "Amen, amen, I say to you, no one can see the kingdom of God without being born from above" (John 3:3). The Greek word *anothen* can mean either "born again" or "born from above," and many versions use the second translation. For our purposes it doesn't matter. But while Fundamentalists make use of this verse to justify their insistence on an internal "born-again" experience, it is curious that they ignore what Jesus says only two verses later: ". . . no one can enter the kingdom of God without being born of **water** and Spirit" (3:5). It is clear from history that the early Church interpreted that text as referring to Baptism, especially when reading it in the light of Jesus' final words, when He commissioned the apostles, "Go, therefore, and make disciples of all nations, **baptizing** them in the name of the Father, and of the Son, and of the Holy Spirit" (Matthew 28:19). Moreover, the Acts of the Apostles and the letters of Paul and Peter are filled with references to the importance of Baptism for salvation; for example, Acts 2:38; 10:44-48. It is certainly true that Baptism without an internal conversion to Christ would be useless for salvation; but it seems equally clear from the Scriptures that, ordinarily, Baptism must accompany the interior conversion.

One question yet remains: Why do Catholics put so much stress on the Baptism of infants? Babies cannot possibly make a conscious decision for Christ. Here is an example of Catholics relying on tradition as well as on Scripture for guidance — although, even in Scripture, there are instances in which whole families received Baptism, presumably some of them being young children (Acts 16:15, 33; 1 Corinthians 1:16). At any rate, Christians began the practice of baptizing children and infants in the first centuries. They believed that Baptism joined them to Christ in a profound and radical way and filled them with the gifts of the Holy Spirit. Why should that wonderful grace be denied to children? Besides, infant Baptism was a powerful way to proclaim the truth that we do not **earn** our salvation; it is purely God's gift. For here is this little child, having "accomplished" nothing as yet, being told by God, "You are my child, my beloved, in whom I take delight" (Cf. Matthew 17:5).

However, Catholics are aware that Baptism is only the beginning of salvation. They agree with Fundamentalists that at some point in our adult life, we must make a conscious commitment or decision for Jesus Christ. The mere ritual of Baptism will not save us unless we internalize its meaning: "I belong to Christ. I want to live for Him, not for myself." In his fine little book *The Born-Again Catholic,* Albert Boudreau says that what we need to do is place Jesus at the **center** of our lives, not just leave Him at the margin or as "one of many" concerns we have. Many Catholics have told me that this is exactly what they experienced on a retreat, or a Marriage Encounter, or a Cursillo, or a parish mission or in the silence of their own hearts. In fact, most mature Catholics say they need to commit themselves to Christ, not just once, but over and over again. The reason for this is not that they don't

Catholics believe that infant Baptism is a powerful sign that we do not earn our salvation; it is God's gift.

believe they are "saved"; it is simply that they are weak, or they forget, or they are influenced by the un-Christian attitudes and values of the society around them.

To speak of salvation as an ongoing process rather than a single event implies something else: Christians have to keep struggling to overcome the forces of sin in self and society, and keep bringing more and more of their life choices into harmony with their commitment to Christ. Fundamentalists tend to dismiss this notion of ongoing effort and struggle as "salvation by good works" instead of by faith. But Catholics do not claim that they are saved by their own works; they know very well that only the death and resurrection of Jesus has power to save them. Yet they see in the Bible a very clear connection between **belonging** to Jesus Christ and **acting** in accord with His teachings. Several passages promote this idea, including the following.

- "If you love me, you will keep my commandments" (John 14:15).
- "Not everyone who says to me, 'Lord, Lord,' will enter the kingdom of heaven, but only the one who does the will of my Father in heaven" (Matthew 7:21).
- The Last Judgment scene, in which Jesus says that our entrance into heaven or hell will depend on the extent to which we tried to respond to the needs of our brothers and sisters, for it is really He whom we serve in them (Matthew 25:31-46).

In a word, "good works" are simply our attempt to live in obedience to the will of Jesus our Savior.

We also need to say a word about how certain we can be of our salvation. The way Catholics understand biblical teaching, we can have a firm **hope** of salvation, but not absolute **assurance.** The Bible gives many indications that even committed believers have the potential to slip away from fidelity to God; therefore, we need what Catholics call "the grace of final perseverance." Some examples from Scripture include the following.

─────────────

- In talking about the last days, Jesus says there will be a host of physical and moral evils coming upon the world, so that believers will be severely tested: "and because of the increase of evildoing," He says, "the love of many will grow cold. But the one who perseveres to the end will be saved" (Matthew 24:12-13).
- "... work out your salvation with fear and trembling," Saint Paul says (Philippians 2:12). Why would Paul say that, if our salvation were absolutely assured? I have often wondered how Fundamentalists interpret that statement.
- Paul himself did not claim absolute certainty about his salvation. In one passage he compares the Christian life to a running race, although the prize is nothing less than eternal life. But he ends up with this remarkable statement: "... I do not run aimlessly; I do not fight as if I were shadowboxing. No, I drive my body and train it, for fear that, after having preached to others, I myself should be disqualified" (1 Corinthians 9:26-27).

─────────────

I really like what Alan Schreck has to say about this topic of salvation in his excellent book, *Catholic and Christian*. He says a Catholic should be able to give a triple answer to those who ask, "Are you saved?" First, he says, a Catholic can say, "Yes, I have been saved." It is an objective fact that Jesus Christ has died and risen to save me from my sins. This salvation has already begun to take effect in the life of everyone who has accepted Christ and received Baptism. Second, Catholics need to say, "I am being saved." I am still "running the race" to my final destiny in heaven. I have to turn to God each day for the grace to enter into God's plan for my life and to accept God's gift of salvation more fully. And third, Catholics can say, "I hope to be saved." We have to persevere in our faith in God, in our love for God, and in obedience to God's will until the end of our lives. We have confidence that God will give us that grace, and that we will accept the gift of salvation until the day we die, although we are always conscious of our human frailty and our need for healing.

As someone has pointed out, Fundamentalists seem to confuse "salvation" with "justification." That is, we are justified, "made right" with God when we acknowledge Jesus Christ as our Lord and Savior and receive Him into our hearts. But "being saved" is an ongoing, lifetime process of conversion, struggle, backsliding, re-commitment, seeking forgiveness, and overcoming our demons. And always, always we know that we are not alone: ". . . I am with you always," Jesus said, "until the end of the age" (Matthew 28:20).

The Second Coming of Christ

A final issue in the question of salvation is the Second Coming of Christ. People have often noted how preoccupied Fundamentalists seem to be with the end of the world. They scrutinize the Book of Revelation and believe that they can find all sorts of clear indications that the end of the world is imminent. This gives added fervor to their evangelizing: They want to save as many people as possible before it is too late.

Fundamentalists will talk a good deal about what they call "the rapture" (although this word is found nowhere in Scripture). The rapture, in turn, is connected with "the millennium," when Christ is supposed to return with His saints to rule over the world for a thousand-year period. Fundamentalists believe that they find this teaching in Revelation 20:2-6, which speaks of Satan being tied up "for a thousand years" and the saints reigning with Christ for the thousand years. Present-day Christians, then, are living in the "pre-millennium," the time just preceding the millennium. We will surely hear these ideas expressed more and more as we approach the year 2000.

This "pre-millennialist" theology is summarized very clearly by Kathleen Boone: "Pre-millennialists believe the literal, historical deterioration of the earth will culminate in a seven-year period of **tribulation,** the horrific details of which are culled from the books of Daniel and Revelation. The tribulation, an outpouring of divine wrath and judgment, will close with the Second Coming of Christ, who will then reign on earth during the millennium. Believers, however, will not suffer through the tribulation. In an event termed the Rapture, Christ will return to gather his saints from the earth immediately prior to the onset of the tribulation. They will return with Christ to reign with him on earth during the millennium. . . . The Last Judgment occurs with the close of the millennium, with all persons sent to their respective eternal destinations" (*The Bible Tells Them So,* pp. 52-53).

It is not difficult to see the implications of this theology. Fundamentalists can find both fear and comfort in it. On the one hand, it is frightening to think about the horrors and disasters that will afflict the earth during "the tribulation"; on the other, it is comforting to think that, since I belong to the company of "the saved," I will be "raptured out" of the tribulation and enjoy a peaceful reign with the Lord.

The other implication has to do with how I spend my time on this earth. If the world is inevitably headed toward moral deterioration and eventual destruction, it is futile to spend my energy in trying to reform it. Rather, I should devote all my efforts to bringing people to make their decision for Christ, so that they will be ready for the rapture. This is why, for example, Jerry Falwell says, "Paul did not get sidetracked into social reform. One cannot transform a lost society. The Gospel will transform individuals in society, and this is the minister's calling." And evangelist Bob Jones tells his flock: "The church is not in the world to bring peace. The Gospel is a sharp, two-edged sword. Christ's commission to His disciples is to preach the Gospel. . . . The church is not told to change the moral climate of the world. The commission of the church is to save men and women out of the world. Anyone who knows and believes the Scripture recognizes that the moral situation of the world is going to grow worse and worse as we go further and further into the apostasy."

However, Fundamentalists do not seem to follow this theology consistently. Logically, we would expect them to maintain a posture of distance and noninvolvement in political and social concerns, as their verbal rhetoric indicates. Yet Jerry Falwell has founded the "Moral Majority," intended to "change the moral climate of the world." Pat Robertson has a clear political agenda and was even a candidate for the presidency. Other Fundamentalist leaders urge their followers to oppose legal abortion, the Equal Rights Amendment, and so on. There seems to be some sort of contradiction here.

In any event, Catholics have quite a different understanding of their role in the world and their attitude toward the future coming of Christ. They believe that Jesus surely will come at the end of time to judge the whole human race and to establish the definitive reign of God over all human history. But it is clear from Scripture that no one knows the exact time that this will occur. Several times Jesus said things like this to His disciples: "But of that day or hour, no one knows. . . . Be watchful! Be alert! You do not know when the time will come. . . . Watch, therefore; you do not know when the lord of the house is coming. . . . May he not come suddenly and find you sleeping. What I say to you, I say to all: Watch!" (Mark 13:32-37). From the context, it is clear that Jesus is speaking both of our individual "hour" (our death) and the "great tribulation" that will precede the end of the world.

As for the millennium, most Catholic and Protestant biblical scholars do not believe that the "thousand years" in Revelation 20 should be taken literally. It refers to a long period of time during which Christians will experience a great deal of peace and freedom, as though Satan's power is bound up

Catholics and Fundamentalists hold differing views about the future coming of Christ.

and the teachings and presence of Jesus seem to hold sway in the world. Perhaps this period has already taken place, as in the fourth century when the persecutions ceased and most of the Roman Empire became Christian. Or perhaps it is still to come. At any rate, the scholars see no evidence for the rapture or for a literal thousand-year reign of believers with Christ. As a matter of fact, the text says that those who are to reign with Him are those who have already died (Revelation 20:4). There is nothing about the living being "raptured out." Paul does speak of those who are alive being "caught up together with them [the dead] in the clouds to meet the Lord in the air" (1 Thessalonians 4:17), but he is clearly talking about the final coming of Christ at the end of time.

Meanwhile, Catholic teaching has consistently maintained that believers are called to be involved and concerned about the state of the world. This theme is very clear in the Bible. We have already seen that Jesus tells us that we will finally be judged by the way we have responded to our brothers and sisters who were in need (Matthew 25:31-46). In the story of Lazarus, the rich man was sent to hell, not because he was rich, but because he had no concern for the poor man at his doorstep (Luke 16:19-31).

In the parable of the talents, the man with the one talent is condemned by his master, not because he had only one talent, but because he did nothing with it (Matthew 25:14-30).

It seems evident that Jesus is telling us that we are responsible for each other's well-being, physical as well as spiritual. And, because people have to live in society, we need to take care that the society will be supportive rather than

According to Catholic teaching, believers are called to be involved and concerned about the state of the world.

destructive of their physical and spiritual good. As Peter wrote to the early Christians: "As each one [of you] has received a gift, use it to serve one another as good stewards of God's varied grace" (1 Peter 4:10).

This notion of Christians as "good stewards" of the earth and its people is a major theme in Catholic social teaching. One hundred years ago (1891) Pope Leo XIII wrote his great encyclical *Rerum Novarum*, "On the Reconstruction of the Social Order." He set forth clear principles for the building of a just social order that would correct the evils of both unbridled capitalism and godless communism. The Second Vatican Council urged all Catholics to work together to build a more just and peaceful world: "It is a mistake to think that, because we have here no lasting city, but seek the city which is to come [heaven], we are entitled to shirk our earthly responsibilities" *(Pastoral Constitution on the Church in the Modern World,* article 43).

Note how careful the bishops are not to split our spiritual life from our temporal life. Later in that same text they say very forcefully that there must be "no . . . opposition between professional and social activity on the one hand and religious life on the other. The Christian who shirks his temporal duties shirks his duties toward his neighbor, neglects God himself, and endangers his eternal salvation." Those are strong words indeed. But this has been the Catholic position throughout history. We take this world very seriously, because it is God's handiwork and the arena in which we are to grow in holiness and find our salvation. Our final destiny is heaven, but we are not to be "standing there looking at the sky," as the angels said to the first apostles (Acts 1:11). Nor do we withdraw from the world because it seems to be getting more corrupt all the time. Rather, we devote our energies to sharing the Good News about Jesus Christ and working to bring about His reign in our world. A wonderful vocation indeed.

CHAPTER FOUR

How Can We Respond to Fundamentalism?

I am writing this book primarily for Catholics who are seeking a better understanding of Fundamentalism, although I am hoping that Fundamentalists themselves will read it and come to a better understanding of Catholicism. I am also aware that many Catholics are wondering how they themselves or their parishes can meet the challenges that Fundamentalism offers to our Church and its members. First I would like to present some suggestions for parishes, then for families and friends of Catholics who have already joined Fundamentalist churches.

How Can Our Parishes Respond?

In the earlier part of this book I noted a number of elements in Fundamentalism that have a strong appeal. One of them was the emphasis on the Bible. Some Catholics say they do not find this in their own Church. What can we do to offset this perception? For one thing, we priests need to dedicate our energies to solid biblical preaching. Our people are hungry to be nourished by the word of God. It is not enough just to repeat the Scripture texts that were read at the Mass and make a couple of obvious applications to life. We have to dig into the text, ponder it, wrestle with it, pray over it until it seeps into our bones. Then we make connections between the sacred text and the lives of our people. We may shake our heads in dismay over the simplistic way the Fundamentalist preachers make use of Scripture. But they have one thing that many of us seem to lack: passion for the word of God. People are touched and moved by solid, passionate biblical preaching. I find myself more and more taking the Bible or the Sunday missal into my hands while I am preaching, so I can easily find and read the text when I want to. Also, I no longer like to stand behind the pulpit while preaching; I want to move about freely with a walk-around microphone. I want to do whatever I can to make that word of God come alive in the hearts of my listeners.

Another direction we need to continue moving in is Bible study. This is the one adult education "program" that seems to be most successful in parishes, and it is getting more and more common. But there are still too many places where it is nonexistent. Or, if it is in place, it is too often an intellectual "head-trip" instead of a search for deeper faith and commitment.

At the same time, our Catholic people must not slip into the "Bible-alone" mentality of Fundamentalists. As I tried to show earlier, we Catholics have always linked the Scriptures together with tradition for a wholistic understanding of our faith. But here I wish to make another point. It seems to me that Fundamentalists claim to meet God in only one way — in the Bible. It is an interior, invisible encounter between God and the individual soul. We Catholics agree that this is one way — a privileged way — that God comes to us. But we believe that there are other ways — the external, visible signs that we call "sacraments." In the first place, Jesus Christ Himself is **the** sacrament of God; that is, through His taking on a human nature the invisible God has become visible (1 John 1:1-3). Moreover, the New Testament shows that Jesus continues His presence in the world visibly through the Church. That is why Jesus could say, "where two or three are gathered together in my name, there am I in the midst of them" (Matthew 18:20); His invisible presence is manifested in the visible gathering of believers in faith. For the same reason, Jesus gave His church the authority to speak in His name: "Whoever listens to you [the apostles and their successors] listens to me. Whoever rejects you rejects me" (Luke 10:16). In a mysterious but real way, Jesus continues His presence in the world visibly through the Church.

Moreover, in the New Testament we see that Christians make frequent use of external signs and rituals in the belief that God works powerfully through them. We have already seen their widespread practice of Baptism, an external washing whereby they believe they are cleansed, transformed, "reborn" into newness of life in Christ. But we see them using other signs and rituals also: The apostles impose hands on people, and they receive the gifts of the Holy Spirit (Acts 8:17); if there are sick members, the "presbyters" are called in to pray over them and anoint them with oil so that they may recover (James 5:13-15). And Christians gather regularly to celebrate "the Lord's Supper," in which they believe they receive the body and blood of the Lord Jesus Himself: "The cup of blessing that we bless, is it not a participation in the blood of Christ? The bread that we break, is it not a participation in the body of Christ?" (1 Corinthians 10:16).

This matter of the Eucharist, the Mass, has been a great source of controversy between Fundamentalists and Catholics. Fundamentalists say that the Mass is contrary to the Scriptures, which insist that Jesus offered only one perfect sacrifice for our sins; to keep offering more sacrifices is equivalent to idolatry. They quote the passage in Hebrews that says: "For Christ did not enter into a sanctuary made by hands, a copy of the true one, but heaven itself, that he might now appear before God on our behalf. Not that he might offer himself repeatedly, as the high priest enters each year into the sanctuary with blood that is not his own; if that were so, he would have had to suffer repeatedly from the foundation of the world. But now once for all, he has appeared at the end of the ages to take away sin by his sacrifice" (Hebrews 9:24-26).

At first glance this looks like a strong argument against the Catholic Mass. However, the context makes it clear that the author is merely contrasting Christ's sacrifice with the Old Testament sacrifices, which had no power to take away sins. He certainly is not talking about the Eucharist. Moreover, it is clear from both Scripture (1 Corinthians 11:17ff) and from history that Christians gathered to celebrate the Eucharist at least weekly, and that they believed they were doing so in obedience to the command of Jesus to "do this in memory of me" (Luke 22:19). Furthermore, they believed they were mysteriously (sacramentally) re-enacting the one perfect sacrifice of Jesus and were partaking of His true body and blood. How else could Paul make such strong claims? "For as often as you eat this bread and drink the cup, you proclaim the death of the Lord until he comes. Therefore, whoever eats the bread or drinks the cup of the Lord unworthily will have to answer for the body and blood of the Lord" (1 Corinthians 11:26-27).

In his wonderful book *Catholic and Christian,* Alan Schreck has a fine discussion of this matter. The Catholic Church, he says, has never taught that in the Mass Jesus is "re-sacrificed" or offered up to suffer again. Rather, the Mass is called a sacrifice because in it the one sacrifice of Christ on Calvary is made real and present to us by God, through the visible signs of bread and wine, so that we can enter into this central mystery of our faith in a new way (pp. 133-34).

Catholics take the doctrine of the Incarnation very seriously. Just as God has come close to us in the human form of Jesus Christ, so God continues to come to us in other visible forms: the words of Scripture, the sacraments, other persons. Sometimes these forms seem very fragile indeed — which is why we need to pray for faith to see the gracious, loving face of God hidden within them.

Catholics find God in the words of Scripture, in the sacraments, and in people.

Personal Relationship with Christ

I would like to suggest another direction we Catholics need to move in. One of the strengths of the Fundamentalist churches is their stress on the importance of having a personal relationship with Jesus Christ. For them, Jesus is not only their Savior; He is also their friend. They are not satisfied with a "heady" religion, but one that appeals to the heart. Catholics, on the other hand, sometimes feel that their religion is too impersonal, intellectual or ritualistic. They are attracted by the Fundamentalists' appeal to "commit your life to the Lord Jesus." As we have seen, this can sometimes be an escape from the hard moral demands of the Gospel. Still, it strikes a responsive chord in the hearts of many Catholics.

I will never forget a statement I once heard from a Catholic prelate, Bishop Raymond Lucker. He said, "Too many Catholics have been catechized and sacramentalized, but never evangelized. They have never heard the Good News of Jesus Christ. And I don't blame them," he said. "We taught them for years that you become a Catholic by learning a set of doctrines and following a set of rules. But we never taught them to **know the Lord.**"

At its best, the Catholic tradition has always placed the personal relationship with Christ at the center of religion and spirituality. The goal of the Christian is **union with God** through Jesus Christ. In the Gospel Jesus says so clearly, "I am the way and the truth and the life. No one comes to the Father except through me. If you know me, then you will also know my Father. . . . Whoever has my commandments and observes them is the one who loves me. And whoever loves me will be loved by my Father, and I will love him and reveal myself to him" (John 14:6-7, 21). Note the stress on the intimate, personal relationship between Jesus and the individual, as well as His insistence that love is revealed in **action** (keeping His commandments) not merely in feeling.

It may be that we in the Catholic Church have lost some of that deep sense of personal relationship with Jesus Christ. We have been preoccupied with revising the Liturgy, changing Church structures to include greater lay participa-

tion, and motivating people to get involved in social justice
issues. These are all necessary, but we always need to take care
that we do not lose our Center. Could it be, for example, that
we need to revive what used to be called "popular devotions"?
We abandoned these because we wanted to restore the central-
ity of the Mass — surely a correct goal. But my sense now is
that the Eucharistic Liturgy is not meeting all the spiritual
needs of all our people. Perhaps we need to restore some devotions like Holy Hours, Forty Hours' Adoration, scriptural
prayer services centered on the Sacred Heart of Jesus, or on
the life of Mary, or on healing for our personal hurts and family problems. Some parishes are already experimenting with
forms of devotional prayer and find that they are satisfying
real hunger in many people.

Something else we can surely learn from the Fundamentalist churches is the importance of being a warm and
welcoming parish community. I was once having lunch with a
priest friend in a crowded restaurant on a Sunday noon. He
and I were both in retreat ministry at the time, so we were
"talking shop" about preaching, prayer leadership, and so on.
At the table next to us was a young couple with two beautiful
children, and I could see that they were somewhat straining to
hear our conversation. Finally they came over and said,
"Excuse us, but we can't help overhearing your discussion; are
you preachers?"

"Yes," we said, "we're Catholic priests."

"Great!" they said. "We've just been to church at the
Assembly of God. Our pastor is so wonderful. He keeps telling
us how we need to confess our sins. We have Bible study every
week. Now he wants to build a school so our children can have
a good Christian education. Isn't that wonderful?"

We assured them it was, and as the conversation went
on they let us know that they "used to be Catholic." Finally I
spoke up: "Tell me something. You say you once were Catholic,
and now you're moved by the need to confess your sins — yet
we've always had confession in the Catholic Church. We've
always had schools for our children, and lately most parishes
have begun Bible study. Could you tell me: What was missing
in the Catholic Church that you're now finding in the Fundamentalist church?"

Their answer surprised me by its simplicity. "The Catholic Church," they said, "was so cold! Nobody talks to you, nobody smiles, and they'd just as soon run you over when they drive out of the parking lot after Mass! Now at our church, everyone smiles and says, 'Hi, welcome! Good to see you! Have you met our pastor yet? We'll introduce you. Have you heard about our new program for . . .?' "

I knew what they were saying, and I felt sad. With a little attempt at warmth and welcome, we might still have had this couple walking with us. And I've heard enough stories like this to make me realize that they were not unique. The good news is this: There's nothing to prevent our parishes from moving in the direction of greater hospitality. In a society where people are constantly on the move, it is becoming more and more important that newcomers be welcomed and helped to feel at home in the parish community. And not only newcomers. As families break up and the number of single people increases, it is urgent that our parishes become places of warmth and welcome.

Catholics Evangelizing?

In this connection, there is something else we can catch from the Fundamentalist churches: their evangelizing spirit. Many Catholics are confused and even intimidated by the term *evangelization*. It calls up images of front-door arguments with Jehovah's Witnesses, Bible-toting televangelists, and radio preachers telling listeners how wrong Catholics are about their beliefs. At the very least, most Catholics are put off by the thought of trying to convert their non-Catholic friends or co-workers.

Much of the negative reaction stems from confusing the idea of "evangelizing" with "proselytizing." Proselytizing is using heavy-handed tactics to persuade others that their beliefs are wrong and ours are right — therefore, they had better join us. That is not what we are talking about. Evangelizing simply means sharing with others our beliefs about Jesus Christ and **inviting** them to take a look for themselves. Our purpose is not to "make converts" or recruit people for the Church, but to be obedient to the command of Jesus: "Go into the whole world and proclaim the gospel to every creature" (Mark 16:15; see also Matthew 28:18-20).

Think of the early Christians. They simply took it for granted that the good news had to be shared. They would go out and meet their family and friends, who would say to them, "What happened to you? You've changed." And the new Christian would say, "You're right — I've come to know Jesus Christ!" And the friend or family member would say, "Tell me about Him." That's how the Christian faith spread. There weren't a lot of mass conversions; there were many more of these one-to-one connections between people. That's why in his letters Paul so often praises the Christians for the fact that "The word of the Lord has echoed forth from you resoundingly" (1 Thessalonians 1:8), and that their faith is being talked about everywhere. Clearly these Christians were not just keeping the faith, they were spreading it; and Paul was proud of them.

I think that one reason we Catholics have been reluctant to evangelize in our own time is that we were not given much encouragement to do so. We've come to think that our religion is pretty much a private matter — something "between God and me" — and I don't "wear it on my sleeve," except maybe in church. Yet, as long ago as 1975, Pope Paul VI wrote a powerful encyclical, *On Evangelization in the Modern World*. In it he reminded Catholics that evangelization is the Church's "primary and essential mission," and that **every** believer, not just the priests and bishops, are called to spread the Gospel. "It is unthinkable," he said, "that a person should accept the Word [of God] and give himself to the Kingdom [of God] without becoming a person who bears witness to it and proclaims it in his turn" (article 24).

Here we do not have space to discuss all the ways that this can be done. But I am convinced that if we start to ask God in prayer to show us how we might begin to evangelize, our prayer will be answered. It is important to remember that there are many people in our own environment who are spiritually lost and searching, often unconsciously, for something to believe in. Many of them (some 16 million in the United States alone) are baptized Catholics who no longer practice their faith. Yet recent research has shown that more than one-third of these Catholics would like to return, but don't know how to go about it. If someone would simply reach out to them in genuine care, lend them a listening ear, and invite them to come back, they would respond.

Here is another simple way to evangelize: When we try to be good listeners, people often open up to us. When they talk to us about some problems or some painful situation in their lives, sometimes we just know it's the right moment to share with them our faith in Jesus Christ. We can offer to pray with them, right there. We can tell them about a time in our lives when we went through something similar, and we experienced God's help in a very beautiful way. We can invite them to come with us to Mass or to our Bible study group. We don't argue; we don't pressure. We simply share what we have experienced. If we are prayerful people, God will show us when and how to evangelize, and God will give us the courage to do it. The past few years I have been teaching a semester-long course on evangelization to seminarians, as well as a shorter training program on one-to-one evangelization for lay Catholics. I have been heartened by the interest and enthusiasm people develop when they get into this topic.

In conclusion, I would like to offer a few thoughts for those Catholics who have family members or friends who have joined Fundamentalist churches. In the very first place, what-

It is urgent that our Catholic parishes become places of warmth and welcome.

ever else you do, continue to love them. Do not reject or dis-
own them, no matter how hostile they may have become. In
some extreme cases, of course, you may have to forbid them to
enter your home if they are upsetting or pressuring your own
children. But continue to pray for them and treat them
lovingly.

Second, try to affirm whatever good you see happening in
their lives because of their involvement in the Fundamentalist
church. Sometimes it will be obvious that they are becoming
more prayerful, more faith-filled, more devoted to God and to
Jesus Christ. Perhaps they have become more responsible,
more conscientious as parents, more thoughtful of others and
less self-centered. They may seem genuinely filled with joy and
peace. It would be wrong to "knock" any of this just because
they found it outside the Catholic Church. These could all be
what Paul called "the fruit of the Spirit" (Galatians 5:22-23).

On the other hand, do not hesitate to challenge what
you see as objectionable or inconsistent with true Christian
principles. As I mentioned in the first chapter, Fundamentalist
believers can sometimes be almost cruel in their self-
righteousness and intolerance of others. These and other
unloving behaviors are surely out of place in one who claims to
be a follower of Jesus. Sometimes, too, you may be able to
show them how they are becoming unbalanced: for example,
giving so much time and energy to the church that their children's needs are being neglected; so overly zealous about "soul-
saving" that they are turning everyone off and losing friends.
Or perhaps it is evident that they are becoming joyless, grim
and unfree.

Finally, try to avoid getting into arguments with them
about the Bible, what someone called "biblical shoot-outs"! For
one thing, you will never win; they can always come back with
another Scripture quote. For another, you will probably never
succeed in convincing them so long as they are in an argumen-
tative frame of mind. What you can do, though, is ask them
some questions or give them some Scripture quotes and just
ask them to **think** about them. I have already indicated a
number of these biblical issues in Chapter Two. Here are some
examples.

- What makes you think that your interpretation of that passage is the only correct one? Who is your authority?
- Why do you reject the Eucharist when Jesus says so plainly, "unless you eat the flesh of the Son of Man and drink his blood, you do not have life within you" (John 6:53)?
- Why do you insist that good works are useless when the Bible says, "What good is it, my brothers [and sisters], if someone says he has faith but does not have works? Can that faith save him?" (James 2:14)?

Your friends or family members may come back with a quick answer they have learned in their church; still, such questions can be thought-provoking. And if ever they reach a point at which they want to know more about what we believe, or really have a question they want you to answer, assure them that you will track it down and share it with them. As Peter wrote, "Always be ready to give an explanation to anyone who asks you for a reason for your hope, but do it with gentleness and reverence" (1 Peter 3:15-16).

It is always painful to watch those we love rejecting the religious beliefs and values we've tried so hard to teach them. And it is especially difficult when we feel so powerless to do anything. Here is where, I believe, we need to grow in trust. If we have sincerely tried our best, with the insights we had at the time, to give our loved ones a firm grounding in the Faith, then we can entrust them to God with full confidence. Their spiritual welfare is now in God's hands. What more can be asked of us than that we pray for them, give them a good example of Christian living, and continue to love them? God surely desires their salvation even more than we do. May all of us — Catholics, Fundamentalists, all Christians — continue to seek the Lord in sincerity of heart.

Sometimes, when Catholics are challenged by Fundamentalists, they begin to wonder (maybe for the first time in their lives); Why **am** I a Catholic? Or: Why do I **remain** a Catholic? These are good questions to ask, and each person will have to answer them for himself or herself. Let me share with you my own answers to those questions, based on my own convictions as well as on testimony I have heard from other practicing Catholics.

One aspect of Catholicism that appeals to many of us is its rootedness in history. By that I mean: the Catholic Church is the only Christian church that can trace itself back to the time of Christ and the apostles. It gives us a deep sense of history to know that we are spiritually connected, through our common faith, with Peter and Paul, Mary and Martha, the early martyrs, and all the saintly men and women who were nurtured in the Church. In spite of violent opposition and persecution, and even in spite of its own sins and scandals, this Church has endured to the present day. This can be explained, we believe, only by the divine guidance of the Holy Spirit.

Not only has the Church endured — it has grown and spread to all parts of the world, just as Jesus said it would (see Matthew 24:14). The very word *catholic* literally means "universal." The Church has always taken seriously Jesus' command to proclaim the Gospel to all nations; this accounts for its evangelizing and its missionary spirit. People have often noted how, wherever they may be traveling, they can always find a Catholic church somewhere in the area.

This connects with another phenomenon that Catholics find appealing: The Church manages to preserve **unity** amid all this diversity. A crucial danger in any religious movement is that it will become splintered when the founder and first disciples are no longer around. Members begin to disagree on teachings and practices, and before long the camps split up. We noted this earlier, when we were talking about interpreting the Bible. We saw that there is a need for some kind of divinely

The Catholic Church manages to preserve unity amid diversity.

guided authority to ensure that disputes do not become divisions. At the same time, this authority must not become so heavy-handed that it stifles legitimate differences and imposes an artificial conformity. In my experience, Catholics who choose to remain in the Church do so because they find a basic unity on essential issues, along with a healthy sense of freedom and room for different viewpoints and expressions of faith.

Let me mention one final strength that many Catholics find in their Church: a sense of care and compassion. They find that the Church is there — through its ministers — in times of hurt and pain, loss and grief, anxiety and guilt. Of course, the Catholic Church has no monopoly on compassion. And sometimes it has seemed more stern and judgmental than compassionate; whenever it seems so, it tends to drive people away.

But over the long haul, most Catholics believe, the Church has a fairly good record of caring for people's needs. In times of crisis and social upheaval, the Church has tried to direct its resources toward the alleviation of human suffering. The result has been a steady commitment to the works of mercy: the founding of schools and academies, hospitals and nurseries, shelters and meal programs.

Moreover, the Church has not been afraid to address the causes of human misery, even in the face of criticism and opposition. Pope John Paul II is tireless in his defense of human rights and political freedom. In many parts of Latin America today, the Catholic Church is the only voice of protest against the exploitation of the poor and the brutal violence of oppressive governments. In the United States, the Catholic bishops have spoken out forcefully for the rights of the unborn, for the elimination of nuclear weapons, and for restructuring the economy so that it does not work systematically against the poor and against minority citizens.

If I could summarize what I have been saying, I might put it this way. For me and for many people I know, being Catholic means trying to hold together what should not be separated: Scripture **and** tradition; faith **and** works; Bible **and** sacraments; authority **and** freedom; unity **and** diversity; personal salvation **and** concern for social justice. In any case, it is not enough to be a Catholic simply because one was brought up that way. Each of us needs to think it through and make a personal decision. For further reflections on this matter, I would recommend the fine book by Richard Rohr and Joseph Martos entitled *Why Be Catholic?*

In this small book, *Catholics and Fundamentalists: What's the Difference?*, I have tried to show some of the points of agreement, as well as the differences, between Fundamentalist and Catholic beliefs. I hope I have been able to foster a somewhat better understanding of the two approaches. One final thought: While knowledge of the Bible is a wonderful help in understanding our place in the universe, our purpose in life, and God's plan for helping us deal with life's problems — Catholics believe that we still need to use our intelligence and our human reason to live spiritually. Reason and faith work together to help us find answers to the great questions of life. And, when all is said and done, Catholics know that they have to leave room for mystery. God and God's ways are so vast, so far beyond our human comprehension, that we can only stand in awe and exclaim with Paul: "Oh, the depth of the riches and wisdom and knowledge of God! How inscrutable are his judgments and how unsearchable his ways! . . . For from him and through him and for him are all things. To him be glory forever. Amen." (Romans 11:33, 36).

Bibliography

Boone, Kathleen C., *The Bible Tells Them So: The Discourse of Protestant Fundamentalism.* Syracuse, NY: State University of New York Press (SUNY), 1988, paperback.

Boudreau, Albert, *The Born-Again Catholic.* Hauppauge, NY: Living Flame, 1979, paperback.

Flannery, Austin, O.P., gen. ed., *Vatican Council II: The Conciliar and Post Conciliar Documents,* "Dogmatic Constitution on Divine Revelation" and "Pastoral Constitution on the Church in the Modern World." Collegeville, MN: Liturgical Press, 1975, paperback.

Gilles, Anthony, *Fundamentalism: What Every Catholic Needs To Know.* Cincinnati, OH: St. Anthony Messenger Press, 1985, paperback.

Hunter, James, *Evangelicalism: The Coming Generation.* Chicago: University of Chicago Press, 1987.

Rohr, Richard, and Joseph Martos, *Why Be Catholic? Understanding Our Experience and Tradition.* Cincinnati, OH: St. Anthony Messenger, 1990, paperback.

Schreck, Alan, *Catholic and Christian.* Ann Arbor, MI: Servant, 1984, paperback.